Selling Information Security to the Board

A Primer

Second edition

Selling Information Security to the Board

A Primer

Second edition

ALAN CALDER

it gp™

IT Governance Publishing

IT Governance Publishing
IT Governance Limited
Unit 3, Clive Court Bartholomew's Walk
Cambridgeshire Business Park Ely
Cambridgeshire
CB7 4EA
United Kingdom

www.itgovernance.co.uk

First published in the United Kingdom in 2010
by IT Governance Publishing.

ISBN 978-1-84928-053-2

Second edition published in 2016

ISBN 978-1-84928-799-9

PREFACE

This book originated in a seminar that I was invited to give, by its organisers, at the Information Security Exhibition, Infosec 2010, at Earl's Court in London.

Information security practitioners have to sell complex, often technical, solutions to boards and management teams who, in turn, would prefer that they didn't have to pay any attention to information security.

This requires sales skills, and these skills can be learned. Good, honest, skilful sales people are essential for the day-to-day working of commerce and industry. Information security practitioners with sales skills will usually achieve a lot more within their organisations than those that don't.

ABOUT THE AUTHOR

Alan Calder's background is in sales and general management. Although he led the world's first accredited certification to what has become ISO27001, his continued involvement in the information security industry has been on the interface between management and technology, in the management of information security, rather than the technological infrastructure on which it depends.

Alan has written widely on IT governance and information security management. The book he wrote with Steve Watkins, *IT Governance: An International Guide to Data Security and ISO27001/IS027002*, is now in its sixth edition and is the Open University's postgraduate information security textbook.

Alan is the chief executive officer and founder of IT Governance Ltd (which owns the ITGP imprint), and he continues to work widely within the information security management industry.

ACKNOWLEDGEMENTS

Many of the ideas discussed in this book did not originate with me; many of them have, over the years, become so widely known within the sales industry that their origin has been lost. Where I am able to identify the originator of an idea (such as Maslow and his Hierarchy), I have done so.

CONTENTS

Contents

INTRODUCTION

C-suite IT and information security executives have usually attained their responsible positions by being good at the technical aspects of their functions. Their background, schooling and higher education are mostly in science or technology disciplines. They understand information technology, they're usually up to date with the latest threat developments, trends and risks, and they know their way around the network infrastructure. They may have a good understanding of IT-related best practice frameworks, such as ITIL®, COBIT®, PRINCE2® and ISO27001. They understand information risk.

Boards, however, across most business sectors, are mainly made up of people drawn from a wider educational background, and whose business experience is primarily in commercial operations or sales. The chief executive is almost always someone whose career includes at least a significant stint in general operations, sales or marketing. His or her primary interest is the overall performance of the business: top-line growth, customer acquisition and maintenance, new product/service development, and bottom-line progression. The second most influential person in the top team is usually the chief financial officer, or finance director, someone whose primary interest is the financial representation of the business performance.

Other senior directors are usually directly interested in their line of business or area of functional responsibility whether, for example, sales and marketing, or senior divisional roles. Non-executive board members tend also to be there for reasons other than their interest in, or awareness of, emerging technologies: it might be finance or compliance, but it is usually related more to what they can offer around customer acquisition, sales and marketing, or stakeholder management. Other than in technology businesses, few if any members of the senior management team, have a direct role or interest in IT or in IT's role in business operations.

Information technology is fundamental to business performance today. Information and information technology has to be appropriately protected: confidentiality and integrity must be preserved, while ensuring that information and technology resources are available to those who need them to perform their roles. IT and information security requires investment – of money, time and resources – by the business. Decisions about where and how to invest business resources are made by top management, people with little awareness of, and less interest in, something about which you, the technology or security leader, may be extremely knowledgeable, and the benefits of which are, to you, as plain as the nose on your face.

The problem, in a nutshell, is that for the good of the organisation, you have to find some way of getting uninterested managers and directors to understand enough about a potential technology risk to commit money and resources to applying effective controls. This is a problem faced by sales and marketing people every day: it's how your organisation's products and services get (eventually) into the hands of customers.

You're not a sales and marketing professional. You may even think that sales and marketing professionals swim in the shallow end of the relationship pool. A significant part of the senior management team is made up of people with sales and marketing backgrounds and you need to find a way of getting your message to them.

CHAPTER 1: THE SALES PROCESS

'Sales' are a process. A process has inputs and outputs and proceeds according to certain pre- defined steps.

The input into the 'Selling Information Security to the Board' process is a collection of raw information about one or more specific issues and a proposed course of action in relation to those issues. The identified issue could be as broad as 'inadequate information security across the whole organisation' or as narrow as 'our financial results might leak before they are officially released'. The desired output from the process is a decision, by top management, to commit time, money and resources to implementing the proposed solution.

The stages in the internal corporate sales process are:

- Gather inputs – information about the issue
- Identify a prospect
- Understand the prospect's needs and wants
- Craft a proposal that will link features and benefits of your proposal to the prospect's needs and wants
- Present the proposal
- Handle objections
- Close the sale.

This pocket guide provides basic advice to the information security professional on each of these steps in the sales process.

CHAPTER 2: SALES BASICS

The three basic sales concepts that any information security professional needs to understand are:

1. Needs *versus* Wants
2. Features *versus* Benefits
3. AIDA.

Needs *versus* Wants

'Want' can be defined as 'having a strong desire for something', whereas 'need' is usually understood as being 'a lack of something basic or fundamental that is necessary for continuation'. 'Need' is most commonly understood in the context of an individual's shortage of food, accommodation or healthcare.

The salesperson needs to differentiate between these two human drivers. People often do things they need to do, even if there is something else they want to do instead: the organisation, for instance, may need to comply with a law that limits access to its financial information, even though it wants to tell some shareholders what it's up to. At other times, the desire to tell selected shareholders about an upcoming acquisition might be so strong that the organisation (acting, of course, through its directors) ignores its need to comply with non-disclosure regulations.

An organisation that wants to supply online services to the UK's Department of Health needs to comply with the requirements of ISO/IEC 27001; without such compliance, it will not be able to proceed. On the other hand, an organisation that perceives certification to ISO/IEC 27001 as conferring competitive benefit, might proceed because it wants to do so; it certainly doesn't need to.

The salesperson who can differentiate between 'need' and 'want' is able to craft a proposal that is appropriately balanced, in line with the needs and wants of the board of directors.

Features *versus* Benefits

A 'feature' is an attribute or characteristic of a product or service: something it has or does. One feature of some GRC software solutions is that they have an enterprise dashboard. A 'benefit' is a description of the value of a specific feature to its user. The GRC application dashboard enables the Board to see, at a glance, where there are significant control breakdowns and to take action before they turn into costly problems.

People buy benefits, not features. The words that link a feature to a benefit are: 'which means that'. 'This anti-malware solution has hourly updates (feature) *which means that* we are protected from zero-day attacks (benefit).'

Most technology proposals fail because they focus on features, not benefits. The suggestion that people 'buy the sizzle, not the steak' is one of the better metaphors for the idea of selling benefits, not features.

AIDA

AIDA is an acronym. It sets out the four most basic steps in any sale:

A – Attention I – Interest

D – Desire A – Action

You first have to capture an audience's attention, then build interest, and once the audience is genuinely interested in the subject, you can begin to build desire for the solution that you are proposing. Once desire reaches a certain point, action is usually easy to get. You certainly can't get action without having gone through the first three steps and, if you miss a step (e.g. 'Desire'), you'll not get a result.

For each issue on which you want board commitment, you should work out how to take them through these four steps.

CHAPTER 3: SELF-PREPARATION: UNDERSTAND THE BUSINESS

As I said in my introduction, top management is primarily interested in what makes the business work, not in the technology that underpins it. The attention span of individual senior managers can be short and, if their attention is not caught by an issue, they move on to something else without even getting interested in the subject. And if you talk to them in a language they don't understand, you won't even capture their attention.

'Techtalk' is a language the board doesn't understand. Security layers, protocols, OSes (operating systems), petabytes, virtualisation and TLAs (three letter acronyms) all leave the board cold.

If you're going to have a conversation with the board, you have to speak in their language, and focus on the issues that pre-occupy them. In many commercial organisations, for instance, the issues that are front of mind for most executives are:

- Top-line revenue (or sales income).

- Gross margin (the difference between sales income and the direct cost of buying or producing what has been sold).

- The bottom line (or net income, net revenue or just 'profits' – how much of the sales income is left after meeting all overheads).

- Return on investment (also known as ROI – how much is generated by making a specific investment; this might be measured in percentage terms or in absolute terms).

- Product or service quality (as this is fundamental to maintaining the top-line revenue and the gross margin).

- Risk management (identifying and dealing with any external factors that could derail the organisation's plans for increasing its profits).

- Cashflow (ensuring that there is enough money available to meet the organisation's financial obligations as and when they fall due).

- Competition is a key issue for boards. What are our competitors doing? What new products and services are they launching that might impact our top-line revenue and steal our customers? What can we do to steal their customers? Enlightened boards also ask: 'What might we have to change now in order to compete effectively next year?'

- Legal and/or contractual compliance (as a failure in either of these could undermine the ability to generate sales revenue, might lead to a distracting court case or public prosecution, and could play havoc with an executive's career prospects).

- Boards and top management usually think that measurement is fundamental to how they manage the organisation, saying things like: 'What's measured is what gets done'. KPIs (key performance indicators) are the most widely used measurement tool; KPIs can exist for most aspects of corporate performance, and might include ratios like sales conversion rates, sales per square metre, percentage of faults per million manufactured items, and so on. KPIs are only interesting to a board if they really provide a way of assessing whether or not some important part of the operation is performing at the level necessary for the overall achievement of the business objectives.

- Resources and operational capability are another area of concern for boards; they usually seek to have just enough resources available to meet planned activities and, when considering new initiatives, one of their areas of worry will always be the availability of resources and the extent to which a new initiative might divert people away from what they are currently doing.

About once a year, and usually whenever presented with a new strategic initiative, boards will review their corporate vision, mission, values and strategic priorities. It is often simpler to reject a new proposal than to change any of those core components of the corporate identity.

You'll note that information security does not appear on this list.

You are going to have to become familiar and comfortable with the concepts in this chapter if you are to engage successfully with the board on the topic of information security. You will have to become adept at couching information security proposals, to focus on their measurable benefits in improving the top and/or bottom line, measuring risk, advancing corporate objectives, or meeting compliance requirements.

CHAPTER 4: SELF-PREPARATION: SOFT SKILLS

'People buy people first, and everything else second.'

Good sales people recognise this instinctively. Poor sales people are smarmy, incongruent or irritating. Non-sales people don't even try.

So, what sort of people do people buy? The answer is that 'people like people like themselves'. Most people recognise the broad truth of this statement: their friends have similar interests and lifestyles. Most people marry within their culture, social class, religion and racial background. People are just more comfortable with people like themselves.

Your senior management, however, are not necessarily people like you; they may not feel comfortable with you and, if you persist in speaking tech, they may not even understand you. And, if you persist in displaying how much you know about your subject, they'll find you irritating. If you're good at what you do, you're good at what you do: you don't need to show off your technical knowledge all the time. Business managers are not equipped to assess your technical competence. They assume that, because you have the role that you do, you are competent to do your job. What they are interested in is whether or not you can help them to do theirs.

So, how do you get senior management to 'like' you? The answer is not to try to be likable, or to pretend to be like them: all the time we see politicians trying to be like the ordinary person in the street and we find it false, hollow and condescending. You can, however, without being either false or condescending, dress and behave in a way that informs the person with whom you are talking about how you want to be treated. If the executives in your business wear suits, polished shoes and have their hair done regularly, you're unlikely to be taken seriously if you wear Converses, dirty jeans and have unkempt hair. Facial jewellery, neck bolts and other marks of 'individuality' are likely to mark you out as someone 'not like us'. Outsiders rarely get a proper hearing and so, if you want to successfully sell information security to the board, you have to present yourself in a way that enables you to be considered as a possible insider.

Appropriate dress is just a starting point. You need to empathise with your prospect. The truth is that you can't actually begin to empathise with someone until you've made an effort to understand them. The idea that you must walk half a mile in a person's shoes before you can understand their approach to the world is a good one.

There are five tools for understanding other people: who, what, where, when and how. Any one of these five words, put in front of a sentence, creates what is known as an 'open question'. An open question is one to which the answer cannot be either just 'yes' or 'no'.

'Are you interested in my proposal for deploying an IDS?' is likely to get either a 'yes' or a 'no' answer. Unless that is the answer you want, asking this sort of question (a 'closed question') is not a good move.

'What advantages could we get from stopping hackers before they get into the network?' is an open question: one to which neither a 'yes' nor a 'no' would make sense as an answer. Open questions encourage the person to whom it is directed to open up and, in their answer, to provide more information that enables you to start understanding their attitudes, objectives, needs and wants.

It's important, when you've asked a question, to *shut up* and wait for the answer. Rhetorical questions are those which contain their answer – and an emotional charge: 'wouldn't our shareholders want us to protect the network from hackers?' Most senior managers don't like being posed rhetorical questions, mostly because they suspect that the issue is more complex than the question implies.

Ask a question, and then use your eyes and ears in proportion to how many of them you have, in relation to the number of mouths you have: watch for your listener's reactions and listen to their words. Bear in mind that, in most communications, only seven per cent of the message is contained in the words themselves. 38% of the message is conveyed by tonality, and 55% is conveyed by body language. That's why it's so easy for e-mail messages to provoke unintended consequences and misunderstandings, and why telephone selling can be so difficult. Many top managers and top sales people want to meet face to face, because they know that they will only give, and get, the complete communication in that situation.

While some sales people will want to get familiar with a suite of communication skills, most people have a latent talent for recognising people's actual emotions about a subject, from their physical behaviours while listening to a proposition or answering a question. That information should be treated as information: it needs to be explored.

Follow-up questions should attempt to open up areas of concern and discomfort, so that issues can be identified and resolved; other strands of questions should develop areas of agreement and common purpose, as it is from these areas that understanding will grow.

Finally, a word on written communications: senior management expect to see written communications that are syntactically and grammatically acceptable, that follow standard spelling and typographical conventions and which, above all, follow a fairly standard format in terms of structure and layout. While I'll return to the subject of proposal writing later in this pocket guide, it's worth bearing in mind that clearly written communication is important in establishing yourself as a credible contributor to corporate life.

CHAPTER 5: SELF-PREPARATION: BE CREDIBLE

As an information security leader inside your organisation, you have a unique opportunity to establish yourself with senior management in a way that is not open to any outsider.

Management will always listen to their trusted advisers. They won't always follow their advice, but they will usually pay attention when they raise an issue, and will usually be interested to find out why they need to do something about it.

The trusted adviser, in other words, will almost always get through the first two stages in the AIDA sequence by default.

How does the information security professional become a trusted adviser?

A basic facility with business language, together with the requisite soft skills, is the foundation on which an information security professional builds a career track record of being right more often than not, of under-promising and over-delivering, and of consistently aligning information security strategies with business objectives and the corporate risk appetite.

The Boy Who Cried Wolf should be an instructional story for many information security professionals: those who identify threats in every technological development or who always find some new risk to get in the way of taking action today, are playing to senior management's prejudices about what information security people really do. People who find reasons not to do something are very quickly identified, by management, as barriers to progress. They are not trusted advisers.

Do not peddle 'FUD' – Fear, Uncertainty, Doubt (or Disaster). You might successfully sell something to your management once by creating fear, uncertainty and doubt in their minds but, unless the threat about which you frightened them actually comes into existence, and your proposed solution does actually protect the organisation from calamity, you're unlikely to succeed a second time. Most management teams focus on progress, rather than on barriers to progress. If you focus on barriers to progress, you are likely to become increasingly unable to secure the information security investment you believe the business needs but, conversely, you are guaranteed to find yourself on the receiving end of management's ire when something bad does actually happen.

So, don't spend your days crying 'Wolf!' Instead, concentrate on finding solutions to real business problems, maximising return on the investment that has already been made in information security, ensuring that projects move quickly and efficiently to a conclusion and, above all, that users are able to access the information and technology resources they need, as and when they need them. Helping senior managers achieve their own objectives helps you develop potentially important future allies.

At the heart of a trusted adviser's role is a consistent commitment to 'tell it how it is'. By this, I do not mean that you should just 'speak your mind', because balance, perspective, judgement and pragmatism are the human qualities that underpin someone's ability to provide advice that will be valued.

All information security solutions have their pros and cons; you have to present both, balance one against the other, and explain how you arrive at your judgement that it is, 'on balance', better to proceed or not to proceed. Develop an internal reputation for providing a balanced explanation of the business benefits to be derived from deploying a particular solution, together with clarity about the real costs (and we should be talking total cost of ownership – 'TCO' – and not just the purchase or initial investment cost) and possible disruption caused by the deployment, and a clear exposition of the return that the organisation might expect to make on this investment.

Credibility is particularly important around IT- related regulation. Regulatory compliance is an increasingly big challenge for the IT leader: data protection, privacy, PCI DSS, SOX, HIPAA and computer misuse are just some of the legal areas that impact the IT organisation. A compliance failure may have a negative impact on the organisation: cost of remediation, restitution, brand damage, fines, class-action suits and so on. However, the consequences of non-compliance vary between laws, and the steps between identification of a compliance breach and action against the organisation vary from law to law. It is important to understand how enforcement actually works and to include this knowledge in how you explain the compliance aspects of a proposal to the board.

If, for instance, you justified to your board investment in a data leak prevention solution on the basis that the Information Commissioner in your country had been given the powers to audit data protection compliance, but left out the fact that he didn't have the resources to actually carry out more than (say) five audits a year, you would have misled management. If they had known that the likelihood of regulatory action was very low, they would almost certainly not have approved the investment.

They will find out the truth, though, sooner or later and, once they do, they'll never again trust any proposal you put forward.

That's not where you want to be.

CHAPTER 6: SELF-PREPARATION: BUILD A TRACK RECORD

All information security practitioners know, intellectually, that confidentiality, integrity and availability (C, I and A) are the three key principles of information security management. However, most practitioners actually concentrate more, in their day-to-day environments, on protecting confidentiality and integrity. The concept of 'security' doesn't seem to contain the idea of availability.

However, to the business manager, 'availability' is the most important attribute of information. Line managers want to be sure that they, and their people, can access the information they need to do their job, as and when they need it. This business desire for availability often clashes with the practitioner's desire to secure confidentiality and availability, with the result that new information security solutions are often automatically seen, by management, as new ways of making it harder for people in the business to actually do their job: creating sales.

If you want the board to be really open to your trusted advice on information security, you need to be perceived as someone who not only understands that availability is critical, but who consistently delivers improvements in information availability, while ensuring that the necessary security activities take place unobtrusively in the background.

Your mission, in a sense, is to *remove barriers* to the organisation successfully pursuing its business objectives, while simultaneously ensuring that the confidentiality and integrity of valuable information is appropriately protected.

In order to deliver 'enabling' information security, you do have to understand both the process of risk assessment and management, and your own organisation's risk appetite.

There are extensive guides to risk assessment.[1] The principles though are simple. It starts with an identified, valuable information asset, and then it considers the threats that might attack that asset, and the specific vulnerabilities that those threats might exploit in order to attack the asset. Foreign hackers, for instance, are only a danger to your local network if there is an Internet access point they could attack, and if that Internet access point has open ports.

It is not enough simply to identify a threat and vulnerability; there must also be a likelihood of the attack occurring and a meaningful impact on the organisation if it were to be successful. An attack with a low likelihood of occurrence, or one which would have only a minor impact, may not be worth worrying about. Risk assessment is a core skill of information security risk management and it is worth getting, to be good at it.

Understanding your organisation's risk appetite is the next most important thing in this context. Once you can do an effective and useful risk assessment in relation to a specific asset (or assets), you need to be able to determine what your organisation's likely response to the risk would be and, if the response is likely to be 'accept but control', then you need to be able to assess what kind of control is worth putting in place.

Classically, organisations can accept risks (i.e. live with the risk, take no action in respect of it), reject them (i.e. refuse to expose the asset to the threat), transfer them (usually by insurance), or accept but control them. 'Accept but control' means that you select and apply one or more controls in order to reduce either the potential impact or the likelihood to a level that the organisation can tolerate.

A 'control' is simply a countermeasure for a risk; it could be technical, administrative or behavioural in nature. Most controls usually contain all three aspects: an effective firewall, for instance,

---

[1] See, for instance, *Information Security Risk Management for ISO27001/ISO27002*, Alan Calder and Steve Watkins, ITGP (2010).

is a technical implementation, to a documented standard, by an appropriately trained firewall engineer.

It is essential that you understand your organisation's risk acceptance criteria, or their tolerance for risk. All managements know that a certain element of risk is attached to their undertakings, and as long as the risk doesn't become too great, they can live with that risk. This tolerance level varies from organisation to organisation. An information security professional who understands the organisation's risk tolerance, will know whether or not it is worth addressing specific issues. All too often, the information security practitioner gets hung up about controlling a risk that management simply doesn't care about; trusted advisers don't go on about stuff that management doesn't care about. If you think management misunderstand a risk, and you believe that if they did they would not be so tolerant of it, then you have a duty to educate them. Unless that is the case, don't even talk to the Board about risks that won't matter to them, that are within their range of risk tolerance.

Finally, delivery: be sure that you consistently deliver technical and security projects on time, to budget and to specification. Every time you fail on one or more of these, you reduce the likelihood of management signing off on another project; it doesn't matter what reasons you offer for failure, however much some third party might be to blame, management will see you as accountable, and will hold you to account.

If, on the basis of your track record, they believe that you simply can't deliver your proposals, you're not likely to get many approved and, worse, you may sooner or later find yourself looking for employment elsewhere.

CHAPTER 7: DEVELOP AN ALLY

'Sales' is a transaction: on one side is a seller (you) and on the other is a buyer (the board). The board, however, is not an individual – it is a collection of individuals and, in order to sell to a group, you have to understand something about how groups make decisions, and, in particular, how your board works.

Unless you are already a member of the board, or of the senior management group, you're unlikely to have much of an insight as to how decision making works. You need to know, for instance, if your board's decision making is centralised on one individual (usually either the chairman or the chief executive), or whether it is a more inclusive, considered process; otherwise, you could find yourself, for instance, making a presentation to the board as a whole, helping them all get informed, and then see the proposal rejected because the chief executive doesn't agree with you.

So, you need to develop your understanding of how the board makes decisions. The simple starting point is to ask colleagues, both in the IT organisation and elsewhere in the organisation, about their experience with presenting investment or procurement proposals. Talk to those who succeeded, as well as those that didn't, and build a mental picture of how to succeed within the culture of your own organisation. Get as clear a picture as possible about what the board's 'hot buttons' are, find out the risks and concerns that habitually worry them, and try and establish what the board's idea of a 'good proposal' looks like.

You should then seek out one or more allies on the board. You're looking for individuals that you know have similar views to yours on specific issues – they don't have to be friends, or share a wider range of interests, they just have to have similar views on specific information security issues.

Developing a relationship with an ally takes time. All the things that I've talked about in previous chapters of this pocket guide contribute to what you're trying to achieve. In addition, you could perhaps strike up an e-mail relationship with your target allies, in which you send them infrequent updates on significant issues, and how they've been cost effectively dealt with. You could also provide specific updates on emerging issues that affect the industry generally.

These sorts of e-mails should be relatively infrequent, should be with the recipient's initial permission, should not peddle FUD and should not be self-aggrandising. They should give the recipient inside or specialist knowledge that enables them to perform their current role better.

A good ally should be able to give you useful insight into how the board's decision-making process works, and should be able to give you practical advice as to how you should focus your investment proposals, what to include and what to leave out. This is the first significant contribution that a good ally can make to your sales planning.

The second is that they should be able to champion your cause to the board, helping ensure that the subject matter makes it onto the board agenda, that enough time is scheduled to deal with it, and that it will get a sympathetic hearing. Of course, if you are working with someone that everyone else on the board can't stand, their association with you may actually damage your cause.

You need to understand, therefore, what motivates management.

CHAPTER 8: WHAT MOTIVATES MANAGERS?

Officially, managers in the private sector are motivated by their obligation to maximise the return on capital invested in the organisation by shareholders; in the public sector, by a sense of public duty; and in the third or voluntary sector, by a commitment to the cause of their members.

In those (mostly) smaller organisations in which management still holds the largest percentage of the shares (i.e. well over 50%), what management wants is usually in line with what the shareholders want. This is not always the case in larger organisations, where management is, in effect, the agent of the shareholders. There is a body of research which argues that the 'agency effect' is, in fact, detrimental to shareholders.

In larger organisations, you might think that management is motivated by the pursuit of the organisation's vision and mission and will behave in accordance with its values.

Google's published vision, for example, is: 'Organise the world's information and make it universally accessible and useful'. Its mission is a much longer statement, called 'Ten things that we know to be true'.[2] Google's values are summed up in this easily remembered statement: 'Do No Evil'.

The reality is that corporate executives tend to be only indirectly interested in their vision and mission and, while they expect staff to align themselves with the corporate values, they don't always expect the same of themselves.

Experience suggests that corporate executives are driven by much more personal objectives.

---

[2] See: *https://www.google.com/about/company/philosophy/.*

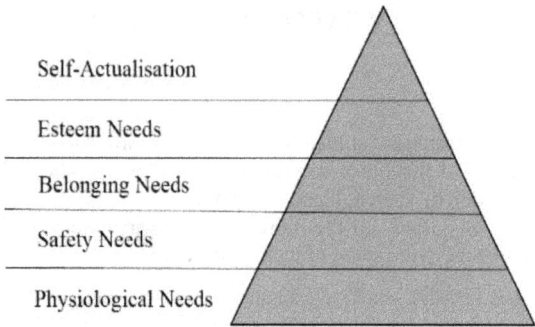

Figure 1: Maslow's Hierarchy of Needs

In 1943, an American psychologist, Abraham Maslow, originated the idea that people had a hierarchy of needs, the lowest of which were the physiological needs – to breathe, eat, sleep, excrete, and so on – and that, once (and only then) a particular level of need was satisfied, they would move up the hierarchy to the next level of need. The pinnacle of the hierarchy was something that he called 'self-actualisation'.

Maslow's Hierarchy of Needs[3] is usually expressed in the form of a pyramid:

Maslow's Hierarchy is useful because it tells you that, at a personal level, corporate executives are likely to be motivated by their need to belong (this is usually more true of junior executives than senior ones), or by their need for esteem. More senior executives are often motivated by what we think of as 'ego', or what Maslow would describe as 'esteem needs': the need for the respect of others, the need for status, recognition, fame, prestige, and attention.

---

[3] There is a straightforward description of the Hierarchy on Wikipedia: *https://en.wikipedia.org/wiki/Maslow%27s_hierarchy_of_needs*.

In larger organisations, you can use the vision, mission and values as leverage in your presentation of an investment proposal but, fundamentally, you need to appeal to the corporate executive's need for esteem; you certainly need to avoid getting on the wrong side of management's collective ego.

You achieve this in two ways. The first is to avoid demonstrating how much cleverer, and better informed you are than the management: senior managers have power and authority and they expect subordinates, however technically brilliant, to remember that they have less power, authority and, therefore, lower status.

The second is to present proposals and solutions to information security challenges in ways that enable senior managers (usually, in this circumstance, your boss or your boss's boss) to claim the credit for them; unless the rest of the management team is half-witted, they will easily work out that the original thinking on your specific information security issue won't have been your boss's. Your competence will, in other words, become known and recognised – and the other senior managers will feel good about themselves for having identified the real talent.

In this way, you can get an information security investment proposal taken forward by a senior manager who hopes to achieve praise/reward from having solved a problem that his or her colleagues hadn't even realised existed, be discovered by the rest of the management team, and get your proposal approved.

Two classic texts worth reading, even though neither was written specifically as guidance for information technology executives, are:

- *The Prince*, Niccolò Machiavelli.
- *The Art of War*, Sun Tzu.

Both texts offer many valuable lessons on how to get things done inside larger organisations.

CHAPTER 9: PLEASURE AND PAIN

Most individual managers are driven by a combination of the desire to experience pleasure and a determination to avoid pain. In the corporate world, pleasure usually materialises as salary increases, bonuses and stock options, while pain is expressed by demotion, public humiliation and possible jail time.

In the experience of most technologists, senior managers and board members have the attention spans of gnats; unless an issue is directly related to improving either the top line (revenue) or the bottom line (profit before tax, or EBITDA,[4] or whatever particular number is your company's obsession), they pay it only the briefest of attention.

All information security proposals, therefore, should, if possible, be couched in terms of how they will either improve revenues (or EBITDA or whatever) or how they will protect revenue (or EBITDA, etc). You can't overtly make the link between a left-to-right, steadily rising graph of corporate earnings and executive compensation, as this is taken as read by most executives.

The reality is that, apart from those information security projects that clearly improve availability of information, few information security projects will contribute directly to rising revenue. Most such proposals are far more likely to remove risks to current and future earnings, or to protect the downside of corporate activity. For instance, it is quite easy to see that tight security around all aspects of a new, breakthrough product will, in the months before launch, ensure that a competitor isn't able to steal a march on you. It is less obvious, but still relatively easy to see that compliance with PCI DSS will ensure that, for an e-commerce business, most of the financial

---

[4] Earnings before interest, tax, depreciation and amortisation.

costs that would come from a successful theft from an unprotected network of large quantities of payment card data, are removed.

The financial implications of a breach of the UK's Data Protection Act, though, are far harder to quantify, not least because there is no legal obligation on a private sector organisation to even report any breaches.[5] Covering up a breach – details about which emerge later – will, however, be dealt with much more fiercely by the Information Commissioner than if they had been reported in the first place. While there may be financial penalties, the size of these penalties may still seem, to some larger organisations, derisory.

If, however, there is a demonstrable link between financial costs and the bottom line, corporate executives are still likely to pay attention. Where bonuses are dependent on achieving specific financial results, it may be possible to present breach costs as avoidable, at *a reasonable price*. A 'reasonable price' should usually be demonstrable as something considerably lower than the potential financial impact if the breach were actually to occur.

While loss of personal earnings, or reduction in personal bonus, are outcomes that most corporate executives will take determined steps to avoid, self-interest as a motivating factor is even stronger where there is the possibility of a significant negative impact on a career. A significant security failure – such as the leak of sensitive financial information ahead of a takeover bid – can lead to formal external investigation and to dismissal. In extreme circumstances, directors, chief executives and chairpersons have been forced to resign as a direct consequence of the organisation's failure to implement appropriate information security measures.

---

[5] Although this seems set to change with the introduction of the EU's General Data Protection Regulation, which will mandate reporting of data breaches and impose significant fines for failures to comply.

No director wants to find themselves contemplating the possible end of a career. If jail sentences became commonplace for the consequences of failures to implement effective information security measures, senior managers would pay significantly more attention to the issue than they do now.

CHAPTER 10: LEVERAGING REGULATORY COMPLIANCE

A well-prepared, well-organised, trusted adviser is likely to gain an audience from senior managers to talk through proposals for enabling the organisation to outperform its competitors, while removing non-compliance risk to the bottom line.

Identify a relevant law or regulation that has IT- related compliance requirements: the UK's Data Protection Act ('DPA'), HIPAA and GLBA in the United States, PIPEDA in Canada, and so on. Identify the gaps between your current actual practice and what the law requires you to do, focusing on the bigger issues, the areas of non- compliance which are likely to trigger the bigger problems. Under the UK's DPA, for instance, the absence of a Fair Processing Notice on all websites is likely to be less of a risk than the absence of FIPS 140-2 encryption on all mobile devices that carry personal data. Identify what you would have to do in order to reduce the risk of a breach to an acceptable level (and, remember, an acceptable level is unlikely to be one of zero risk) and work out the cost, in both capital and revenue terms. Identify and approximately cost any disruptions there might be to the organisation while the solution is rolled out. Rework your proposed solution until its costs are below the likely level of a penalty, plus damages, plus brand value diminution.

Now you can create a proposal for positioning your organisation ahead of its competitors, in terms of it being a safer supplier to its customers as a result of meeting the core requirements of a key law, as well as reducing potential damage to the bottom line, at a cost significantly lower than the damage your solution helps avoid.

Such a proposal, in the UK, would benefit from making your board allies aware of the problem some time ahead of providing them with a solution. This means collecting data. Here is some relevant information about UK data breaches:

- 391 incidents reported to the Information Commissioner's Office ('ICO') in the first quarter of 2015.

- 119 of these incidents were the result of theft of unencrypted laptops, computer discs, memory sticks or paperwork.

- 144 of these incidents were the result of 'mistakes'.

- 90 incidents were enigmatically described as 'Other principle 7 failure', which includes failure to password-protect emails containing personal information, processing personal data on non-business computers, and so on.

You might also want to make your board aware of the ICO's official powers. The ICO can:

- conduct assessments to check organisations are complying with the Act.[6]

- serve information notices requiring organisations to provide the Information Commissioner's Office with specified information within a certain time period.

- serve enforcement notices and 'stop now' orders where there has been a breach of the Act, requiring organisations to take (or refrain from taking) specified steps in order to ensure they comply with the law.

- prosecute those who commit criminal offences under the Act.

- conduct audits to assess whether the organisation's processing of personal data follows good practice.

- levy fines in respect of breaches.

---

[6] Data security incident trends, *https://ico.org.uk/action-weve-taken/data-security-incident-trends/*.

Of course, you would want to make clear that the ICO, at the moment, does not have sufficient resources to fully take advantage of its powers and that it is therefore much more selective in how it goes about its job. More importantly, though, you would want to draw your board's attention to the last item in the list above: the power to levy fines. With effect from 6 April 2010, the ICO has had the power to impose substantial fines, **up to a maximum of £500,000**, on organisations that 'deliberately' or 'recklessly' commit serious breaches of the DPA. It would probably also be worth pointing out that something characterised as a 'deliberate or reckless breach' of the DPA is likely also to impact on executive careers, as well as the corporate bottom line.

This power will be expanded under the EU General Data Protection Act (GDPR), which will enable the ICO, as the supervisory authority, to levy fines of up to €100 million or 5% of turnover, whichever is greater. While it's hard to say that the ICO is toothless, the GDPR will certainly provide it with the power to impose much more notable penalties.

Under the current law, the ICO has provided explicit guidance on how it uses its power to levy fines. It will impose a monetary penalty if:

- a data controller has seriously contravened the data protection principles.

- the contravention was of a kind likely to cause substantial damage or substantial distress.

- contravention must either have been deliberate, or the data controller must have known, or ought to have known, that there was a risk that a contravention would occur.

- the data controller failed to take reasonable steps to prevent it.

The ICO has also said that:

> *Its power will be used as both a sanction and a deterrent against non-compliance with the statutory requirements.*

The words that should worry any senior executive are: 'or ought to have known' and 'failed to take reasonable steps'. From the point at which you draw the Board's attention to weaknesses in your DPA compliance regime, weaknesses that indicate a serious contravention of the principles and which could cause substantial damage or distress, the Board is 'on notice' that it has a problem that must be addressed. Failure to address it could lead to a significant corporate fine, negative bottom-line impact, bonus reductions and, possibly, career damage for individual executives.

You have a proposal to put forward, which (fully costed) will cost the organisation less than it might otherwise lose in fines and other damages, and which would enable the organisation to present itself in a positive light to its customers, employees and suppliers.

CHAPTER 11: LEVERAGING ISO27001

The International Standard for best practice in information security management is ISO/IEC 27001. This standard provides a detailed specification for how an organisation should select information security controls, on the basis of a risk assessment, to counter threats to the confidentiality, integrity and availability of the organisation's information assets.

The Standard is written to be technology neutral and sector agnostic; it is as applicable to large organisations as to small, and to the private sector, the public sector and the third, or voluntary, sector. Any organisation that complies with the Standard can have its management system audited by an accredited third party certification body and will then be able to state publicly that its information security practices are formally certificated as compliant with best practice.

There are many circumstances under which such a certificate might have significant commercial value and the case for pursuing ISO27001 can be made on many levels and for many circumstances. An overriding argument can be built around the general risk environment in which the organization is operating. Such an argument[7] starts like this:

> *Business rewards come from taking risks; managed, controlled risk-taking, but risk-taking nonetheless. The business environment has always been full of threats, from employees and competitors, through criminals and corporate spies, to governments and the external environment. The change in the structure of business value has led to a transformation in the business threat environment.*

---

[7] There is extensive, detailed guidance on how to make this case in *The Case for ISO27001*, Alan Calder, ITGP (2005).

The proliferation of increasingly complex, sophisticated and global threats to this information and its systems, in combination with the compliance requirements of a flood of computer- and privacy-related regulation around the world, is forcing organisations to take a more joined-up view of information security.

Hardware-, software- and vendor-driven solutions to individual information security challenges no longer cut the mustard. On their own, in fact, they are dangerously inadequate.

News headlines about hackers, viruses and online fraud are just the public tip of the data insecurity iceberg. Business losses through computer failure, or major interruption to their data and operating systems, or the theft or loss of intellectual property or key business data, are more significant and more expensive.

Against such a background, a trusted adviser would be able to demonstrate to senior management how an ISO27001-certificated information security management system could position the organisation ahead of its less well- organised competitors and, at a cost considerably less than the potential impact of the significant risks out there, ensure that the bottom line is protected. ISO27001 provides management with a best practice, risk-based, management-directed structure for identifying, controlling and mitigating this wide range of rapidly evolving information risks.

Compliance with ISO27001 can also be used to demonstrate effective compliance with information security laws and regulations which, while precise in what must be done, usually contain little guidance on how it should be done. The UK DPA, for instance, says (at Principle 7 of 8) that:

Appropriate technical and organisational measures shall be taken against unauthorised or unlawful processing of personal data and against accidental loss or destruction of, or damage to, personal data.

ISO27001 is a best-practice model for achieving exactly this objective and the same principle can be applied to data protection legislation[8] elsewhere in the world. In the UK, there is now even a standard that specifically deals with the 'how' of DPA compliance: BS10012, the personal information management system standard.

---

[8] This argument is developed in detail in *Information Security Law: The Emerging Standard for Corporate Compliance*, Thomas Smedinghoff, ITGP (2008).

CHAPTER 12: INFORMATION SECURITY GOVERNANCE

This is a much harder sell but, if the board can be brought to understand that it has a governance responsibility in respect of information security, you will have made the task of selling future information security investment proposals that much easier for yourself.

Here's the argument:

The availability, integrity and confidentiality of its data are fundamental to the long-term survival of any 21st century organisation. Unless the organisation takes a top-down, comprehensive and systematic approach to protecting its information, it will be vulnerable to a wide range of threats, including cyber crime and cyber terrorism, data leakage and insider attacks. These threats are a 'clear and present danger' to organisations of all sizes and in all sectors; responsibility for information risk management, for ensuring that the organisation appropriately defends its information assets, can no longer be abdicated or palmed off on a head of IT or CISO. The board has to take action. It's a part – and a very key part – of the board's governance responsibility.

Information security is a board responsibility

Information security is a governance issue, not merely an IT department functional responsibility. In an environment where it is not commercially sensible to invest in providing security against every possible risk, nor where 100% security is affordably achievable, there are five reasons for this:

- The board has to lay down guidelines as to which of the organisation's information assets are to be protected and the level to which this must be done.

- Only the board can effectively prioritise, and lay down guidelines for, investment in information security.

- Information security is a 'whole business' exercise; effective information security requires a set of controls that integrate technology, procedure and human user behaviour in such a way that the board's security objectives are achieved. Only the board can set out the objectives and requirements for such a cross-organisational management system.

- The whole organisation is at risk in the event of a significant information security breach; the board is directly accountable for the corporate reputation, corporate earnings and corporate survival and the board must, therefore, ensure that appropriate arrangements are made to protect the organisation from information risk.

- It is the board's direct responsibility to ensure that the organisation complies with the various laws of the jurisdictions in which it trades. The growing body of information-related legislation is such that the board now has to be proactive in mandating the implementation of a recognised information security management system that will ensure compliance.

Governance and risk management

The board's job is governance and strategy and, therefore, governing strategic and operational risk is a fundamental board responsibility. There are three operational risks (the best definition of operational risk is still 'the risk of direct or indirect loss resulting from inadequate or failed internal processes, people and systems or from external events'[9]) related to information and communications technology that boards need to consider:

---

[9] *Operational Risk*, a consultative document from the Basel Committee on Banking Supervision in January 2001.

- Loss of proprietary information, with resultant damage to earning power and competitive position.

- Loss of customer and personal data, with resultant damage to commercial and directors' personal reputations, as well as regulatory action, financial and punitive loss, and possible jail time for directors.

- Business continuity disruptions, with resulting damage to commercial reputation and actual trading capability.

The board has to prioritise the risks that are to be defended against, in the light of the organisation's information assets, its business model and its overall business strategy. It has to ensure that appropriate resources are committed to realising and maintaining the risk profile that it has mandated.

Corporate governance codes

Corporate governance codes throughout the world recognise that the management of operational risk is a core board responsibility.

The UK's Corporate Governance Code requires listed companies to annually review their risk management and internal control systems, covering 'all material controls, including financial, operational and compliance controls'.[10] The Turnbull Guidance explicitly requires boards, on an ongoing basis, to identify, assess and deal with significant risks in all areas, including in information and communications processes.[11] Sarbanes Oxley requires US listed companies (and, increasingly, there is a knock-through effect onto their major suppliers) to annually assess the effectiveness of their internal controls, and places a number of other significant governance burdens on executive officers,

---

[10] Corporate Governance Code on Risk Management and Internal Control, Section C.2.3.
[11] Turnbull Guidance, paragraph 20.

including the section 409 requirement that companies notify the SEC 'on a rapid and current basis such additional information concerning material changes in the financial condition or operations of the issuer'. Pillar 1 of the Basel 2 Accord aimed to reduce financial institutional 'exposures to the risk of losses caused by failures in systems, processes, or staff or that are caused by external events'.[12] While the 2008–2010 financial crisis was caused by a significant failure of regulatory oversight, the ambition to counter operational risk is undiminished.

Risk assessment has, over the last few years, become a pervasive and invasive concept: a risk assessment must be structured and formal, and nowadays one is expected in almost every context – from a school outing through to a major corporate acquisition. It is certainly a cornerstone of today's corporate governance regimes. In the context of operational risk, a risk assessment is the first step that a board can take to controlling its risks; the most important next step is the development of a risk treatment plan (in which risks are accepted, controlled, eliminated or contracted out) that is appropriate in the context of the company's strategic objectives.

Information risk

If no one else wanted an information asset, it wouldn't be an asset. Information, to be useful to an organisation, must be available (to those who need to use it), confidential (so that competitors can't steal a march) and its integrity must be guaranteed (so that it can be relied upon). Information risk arises from the threats – originating both externally and internally – to the availability, confidentiality and integrity of the organisation's information assets.

Threats to information security are wide-ranging, complex and costly. External threats include casual criminals (virus writers,

---

[12] BIS Press Release, 26 June 2004.

hackers), organised crime (virus writers, hackers, spammers, fraudsters, espionage, ex-employees) and terrorists (including anarchists). More information security incidents (involving members of staff, contractors and consultants acting either maliciously or carelessly) originate inside the organisation than outside it. Baring, Enron, WorldCom and Arthur Andersen were all brought down by insiders. The HMRC debacle was an insider problem. The indirect costs of these incidents usually far exceed their direct ones and the reputational impacts are usually even greater.

The need for determined action to deal with these risks should be self-evident.

Governance challenges

The governance challenge, though, is clear. A 2014 Ernst & Young survey[13] found that only 14% of information security functions report to the CEO, and that only 5% of organisations have a dedicated threat intelligence team to identify real threats facing the organisation. Ernst & Young summed it up:

Cyber risks are growing and are changing rapidly. Every day, cyber criminals are working on new techniques for getting through the security of organizations, including yours. They are doing this so that they can cause damage, access sensitive data and steal intellectual property. Every day, their attacks become more sophisticated and harder to defeat.

Because of this ongoing development, we cannot tell exactly what kind of threats will emerge next year, in five years' time, or in 10 years' time. We can only say

---

[13] Ernst & Young's www.ey.com/GL/en/Services/Advisory/EY-global-information-security-survey-2014 17th Global Information Security Survey, which in 2014 interviewed more than 1,800 executives across 60 countries.

> *that these threats will be even more dangerous than*
> *those of today. We can also be certain that as old*
> *sources of cyber threat fade, new sources will emerge*
> *to take their place.*

Although we will await the 2024 survey results for some time, anecdotal evidence doesn't suggest that much will have changed. In today's corporate governance environment, boards that take their information security governance responsibilities seriously are likely to be those that outperform; if the majority of organisations continue to shirk their information governance responsibilities, their bottom lines will be impacted and the earning power of their executives will be diminished.

IT governance

Of course, effective information security governance is a subset of IT governance. Organisations that adopt an IT governance framework (following for instance, the international standard ISO/IEC 38500[14]) are far more likely to be organisations in which boards recognise their accountability for information security, and take appropriate action.

A logical approach, therefore, is that information security practitioners work to develop an overall board approach to IT governance[15], on the basis that this will ultimately help them achieve an effective information security governance environment.

---

[14] See *Pocket Guide: ISO/IEC 38500*, Alan Calder, ITGP (2008).
[15] For detailed guidance on implementing an IT governance framework, see *IT Governance: Implementing Frameworks and Standards for the Corporate Governance of IT*, Alan Calder, ITGP (2009).

CHAPTER 13: THE PROPOSAL

Your organisation is likely to have a standard format for making formal proposals for capital expenditure for project approval. You'll probably want to follow the standard format.

We've already dealt with the importance of spelling, grammar and syntax.

There are a number of key elements to any potentially successful proposal that you'll want to ensure yours has. (If your organisation's standard proposal doesn't include these elements, you may want to add them in.)

The first, and most important, is the **executive summary**. The executive summary appears at the top of the first page. It contains a concise, clear summary of the issue that the proposal addresses, the impact of a failure to address it, the essence of your proposed solution, the cost of the solution, and a summary of the business benefits of taking this recommended route. As most   executives will only manage to read the executive summary, (and as they have very short attention spans,) you will want to make this summary   as   effective as you can.

Your proposal will then want to have longer sections dealing with some or all of the following:

- Description of the issue.
- Background to the issue.
- Analysis of the issue (this could cover, for instance, the size of the gap between compliance requirements and the security practices actually in place, or the nature of the security attacks and breaches the organisation is currently experiencing).

- Options for dealing with the issue (ranging from 'do nothing' through to an extreme at the other end of the spectrum – your proposal does not want to be at the extreme) together with their costs.

- Your recommendation (together with more detail on the costs, the possible disruption, deployment challenges and so on, and a detailed description of the features and benefits of your proposal, aligning these with the organisation's business objectives).

- Timetable for action (in which you clarify lead times, and set out how soon you need a decision to be made in the context of the date by when a solution needs to be in place).

- A conclusion (which, in essence, says that you are asking for a decision to proceed with this investment by an identified date).

CHAPTER 14: HANDLING OBJECTIONS

The questions and objections phase is a critical phase in any sales process. It's a good phase. You only get objections if your audience has paid a bit of attention and thought a bit about the issues you've raised. So, you should like objections just as much as you like questions. Do not feel or display defensiveness at this point. Welcome questions and objections: they give you the opportunity to better explain areas that your audience may not have fully understood yet.

There is an important technique to handling questions effectively, and that is to 'ask the question back', just to make sure that you've understood it, to demonstrate that you're paying attention and, sometimes, to either give yourself time to think or, more sophisticatedly, to set up a prepared answer.

A question might be: 'What's the likely cost of delaying action on this issue until the beginning of the next financial quarter?' You could ask it back like this: 'Let me be sure that I understand your question. If we delay the start of the compliance project for two months, what might the impact be on the organisation?' If you get a 'yes' to this, your answer is likely to be: 'There will be two impacts. It will extend by two months the time during which we risk a £500k fine and, secondly, it will increase the initiation costs of project X as we will have to retrain the consultants involved from the old process to the new, rather than getting it right at the outset.'

There may be questions to which you don't know the answer. Acknowledge that these are good questions, and commit to coming back with the information (if possible) before the end of the day/week. Do not attempt an answer if you don't know it; you are, after all, a trusted adviser, focused on helping the board make the right decision.

Do not get involved in an argument over aspects of your proposal. The very old adage, that those who win the argument often lose the sale, is as true of selling information security to the board, as it is in any other situation. You have to find ways of turning objections into questions, and into questions that you can usefully answer, rather than seeing them simply as personal attacks to which you have to respond.

CHAPTER 15: DELIVERY

As soon as you have authorisation to proceed, you get to work.

Communication is at the heart of delivery, where the board is concerned. You want to give the board a regular progress report – what's gone well, what hasn't (keeping it simple and short, of course) and providing measurements that indicate the success of the project.

Approval, authorisation to proceed, is just the first step. A crucial step, yes, but actual delivery – on time, on budget and to specification – is even more important. It's how you demonstrate that the board was right to trust you – and how you prepare them for your next proposal, as you take information security forward in your organisation.

ITG RESOURCES

IT Governance Ltd sources, creates and delivers products and services to meet the real-world, evolving IT governance needs of today's organisations, directors, managers and practitioners.

The ITG website (*www.itgovernance.co.uk*) is the international one-stop-shop for corporate and IT governance information, advice, guidance, books, tools, training and consultancy. On the website you will find the following pages related to the subject matter of this book:

www.itgovernance.co.uk/infosec.aspx

www.itgovernance.co.uk/iso27001.aspx.

Publishing Services

IT Governance Publishing (ITGP) is the world's leading IT-GRC publishing imprint that is wholly owned by IT Governance Ltd.

With books and tools covering all IT governance, risk and compliance frameworks, we are the publisher of choice for authors and distributors alike, producing unique and practical publications of the highest quality, in the latest formats available, which readers will find invaluable.

www.itgovernancepublishing.co.uk is the website dedicated to ITGP. Other titles published by ITGP that may be of interest include:

- Once more unto the Breach
  www.itgovernance.co.uk/shop/p-985.aspx

- The Case for ISO27001:2013
  www.itgovernance.co.uk/shop/p-1667.aspx

- Nine Steps to Success: An ISO27001:2013 Implementation Overview
  www.itgovernance.co.uk/shop/p-963.aspx.

We also offer a range of off-the-shelf toolkits that give comprehensive, customisable documents to help users create the specific documentation they need to properly implement a management system or standard. Written by experienced practitioners and based on the latest best practice, ITGP toolkits can save months of work for organisations working towards compliance with a given standard.

To see the full range of toolkits available please visit:

www.itgovernance.co.uk/shop/c-129-toolkits.aspx.

Books and tools published by IT Governance Publishing (ITGP) are available from all business booksellers and the following websites:

www.itgovernance.eu   *www.itgovernanceusa.com*
www.itgovernance.in   *www.itgovernancesa.co.za*
www.itgovernance.asia

Training Services

Staff training is an essential component of the information security triad of people, processes and technology, and of building an enterprise-wide security culture. IT Governance's ISO 27001 Learning Pathway provides information security courses from Foundation to Advanced level, with qualifications awarded by IBITGQ.

Many courses are available in Live Online as well as classroom formats, so delegates can learn and achieve essential career progression from the comfort of their own homes and offices.

For more information about IT Governance's ISO 27001 Learning Pathway, please see:

www.itgovernance.co.uk/iso27001-information-security-training.aspx.

For information on any of our many other courses, including PCI DSS compliance, business continuity, IT governance, service management and professional certification courses, please see:

www.itgovernance.co.uk/training.aspx.

Professional Services and Consultancy

ISO 27001, the international standard for information security management, sets out the requirements of an information security management system (ISMS), a holistic approach to information security that encompasses people, processes, and technology. Only by using this approach to information security can organisations hope to instil an enterprise-wide security culture.

Implementing, maintaining and continually improving an ISMS can, however, be a daunting task. Fortunately, IT Governance's consultants offer a comprehensive range of flexible, practical support packages to help organisations of any size, sector or location to implement an ISMS and achieve certification to ISO 27001.

We have already helped more than 150 organisations to implement an ISMS, and with project support provided by our consultants, you can implement ISO 27001 in your organisation.

For more information on our ISO 27001 consultancy service, please see: *www.itgovernance.co.uk/iso27001_consultancy.aspx*.

For general information about our other consultancy services, including for ISO20000, ISO22301, Cyber Essentials, the PCI DSS, Data Protection and more, please see: *www.itgovernance.co.uk/consulting.aspx*.

Newsletter

IT governance is one of the hottest topics in business today, not least because it is also the fastest moving.

You can stay up to date with the latest developments across the whole spectrum of IT governance subject matter, including; risk management, information security, ITIL and IT service management, project governance, compliance and so much more, by subscribing to ITG's core publications and topic alert emails.

Simply visit our subscription centre and select your preferences:
www.itgovernance.co.uk/newsletter.aspx.

EU for product safety is Stephen Evans, The Mill Enterprise Hub, Stagreenan, Drogheda, Co. Louth, A92 CD3D, Ireland. (servicecentre@itgovernance.eu)

www.ingramcontent.com/pod-product-compliance
Lightning Source LLC
Chambersburg PA
CBHW071121210326
41519CB00020B/6370